COMPASS
PLAYBOOK COMPANION

A Practical Guide to
Creating Breakthrough Success

Also by Terry Pappy:

14 Days: Loving Life with the Love of my Life

COMPASS Playbook: A Practical Guide to Creating Breakthrough Success

A PRACTICAL GUIDE TO CREATING BREAKTHROUGH SUCCESS • WRITE DRAW DOODLE THINK SCRIPT NOODLE SCRIBBLE PONDER VISUALIZE LIST MIND MAP DREAM STORYBOARD IMAGINE CREATE •

COMPASS
PLAYBOOK COMPANION

TERRY PAPPY

3

Better3

Orlando, Florida

First Edition

ISBN 978-0-9838588-1-2

Printed in the United States of America.

Published by Better3, Orlando, Florida.

This publication is for creative entertainment purposes only. Cover and content created by Terry Pappy.

Visit CompassPlaybook.com for additional **COMPASS** content.

For Dad.
For your love and the freedom to be.

Contents

Acknowledgments xi

A Note to the Reader xiii

Why a Playbook Companion? xv

SECTION ONE: UNDERSTANDING COMPASS **19**

What COMPASS Does 21

What COMPASS Delivers 23

Let's Get Started 24

    STICK FIGURES ENCOURAGED 24

    OPEN YOUR MIND 25

    DOGMA AND FINGER-WAGGING 25

    'IT IS WHAT IT IS' 25

    THE PAST IS THE PAST 26

    HAVE FUN OR GO HOME 27

Engaging the Brain with the Creative Process 28

    STORYTELLING 28

    DRAWING 28

    VISUALIZING 29

The Six Premises 30

    PREMISE 1 - DESIRE 30

    PREMISE 2 - ASPIRATION 31

    PREMISE 3 - BELIEF 31

    PREMISE 4 - FOCUS 32

    PREMISE 5 - INSPIRATION 33

    PREMISE 6 - EMOTION 34

Retraining the Mind 35
The Framework 38
    INQUIRY 38
    MESSENGER 38
    BOND 39
Making the Most of COMPASS 40
Capturing Inspirations 41
Creative Processes 43
    WRITE 43
    STORYBOARD 44
    MIND MAP 44
    DRAW 45
    ACTIVITY 45
    VISUALIZE 46
    CREATIVE PROCESS KEY 47

SECTION TWO: INQUIRY PLAYS 49

PLAY 1: FYOs Rock! 51
PLAY 2: Selfish Pleasures 52
PLAY 3: Feeling Meter 53
PLAY 4: Appreciation 56
PLAY 5: Aspirations 57
PLAY 6: Aspiration Clarifier 58
PLAY 7: Data Gathering 59
PLAY 8: More or Less 60
PLAY 9: Unlimited Resources 61
PLAY 10: Ultimate Career 62

PLAY 11: Angel Investor 63
PLAY 12: Goodies 64
PLAY 13: Globe Trekker 65
PLAY 14: Preference Shaping 66
PLAY 15: Life Experiences 67
PLAY 16: Wouldn't it be Nice if... 68

SECTION THREE: MESSENGER PLAYS **69**

PLAY 17: Increments 71
PLAY 18: Belief Barrier 72
PLAY 19: Belief Turnaround 73
PLAY 20: Belief Celebration 74
PLAY 21: Day in the Life 75
PLAY 22: Environment 76
PLAY 23: The Five Senses 77
PLAY 24: Special Space 78
PLAY 25: Ideal Lifestyle 79
PLAY 26: Day-Trips 80
PLAY 27: Emotional Excursion 81
PLAY 28: POV 82
PLAY 29: Anticipation 83
PLAY 30: I'm So Excited! 84
PLAY 31: Well-Being 85
PLAY 32: Expansion 86
PLAY 33: World Attitude 87
PLAY 34: Community 88
PLAY 35: Encouragers 89

SECTION FOUR: BOND PLAYS **91**

PLAY 36: Focus Shifter 93
PLAY 37: Spontaneity 94
PLAY 38: Great Things 95
PLAY 39: Releasing the "How" 96
PLAY 40: Impact 97
PLAY 41: Inspirations 98
PLAY 42: The Interview 99
PLAY 43: Movement 100
PLAY 44: Me-Time 101
PLAY 45: Head Trip 103
PLAY 46: Mentor 104
PLAY 47: Project Completer 105
PLAY 48: Relationships 106
PLAY 49: Personal Aspect 107
PLAY 50: Conversations 108
PLAY 51: Inspiring Others 109
PLAY 52: What's Next? 110

APPENDIX: COMPASS RESOURCES **111**

COMPASS Community 113
About the Author 115

Acknowledgments

Many authors, teachers, fellow seekers and leaders have greatly influenced the creation of COMPASS. In sincerest acknowledgment to them, I have created an online resource that includes information about their books, programs and purposeful work. Please visit CompassPlaybook.com for links to these leading-edge thinkers and organizations.

To the participants of the early COMPASS Write Shops, the proofers and the Players, thank you for helping me create a more powerful, road-tested Playbook. Your open willingness to participate touched me deeply, and your contributions were invaluable.

A special thanks to the Creative Education Foundation (CreativeEducationFoundation.org), Esther and Jerry Hicks (Abraham-Hicks.com), Landmark Education (LandmarkEducation.com), David Sibbet and The Grove Consultants (DavidSibbet.com and Grove.com) for their inspiration in the creation of this material.

A Note to the Reader

Thank you for being you, for choosing this adventure, and for exploring the ability to create the life you want. Thank you for allowing me to offer a framework that will guide you toward fulfilling your deepest aspirations.

The COMPASS Playbook Companion is more than a guide to creating a richer, more self-expressed life. COMPASS showcases the possibilities you want for your life, the ideas *you* design, and the dreams you've always desired, but for whatever reason haven't been able to materialize.

This framework presents new thinking behaviors that invite inspired action through intentional focus. The resulting flashes of brilliance move you toward your desire faster and with greater satisfaction and fun. You'll find the juiciest part of getting to your dream is just that: getting there.

I see you having what you want and more. I see you learning new ways of looking at your life, of appreciation, of focus, and of carving out and evolving your aspirations as you move toward their fulfillment. I see you thrilled with the journey, and I see you growing, living, and loving life like you never have before.

Thank you for bringing me along.

Terry

Why a Playbook Companion?

Creative processes are just that: creative. While some may prefer the all-in-one, original **COMPASS** Playbook to do their Plays, some may want to use:

- Journals
- Sketchbooks
- Binders
- Planners
- Craft paper and art boards
- Corkboards
- Mixed media and textiles
- Computers
- Tablets
- Smart phones
- Or whatever technology is yet to be created...

The **COMPASS** Playbook Companion provides you more freedom to create, organize and review your Plays the way you want. Since all Plays are re-Playable, you now have the flexibility of using any recording tool, making each **COMPASS** experience distinct.

Create a Playbook binder with the easy 8.5"x11" templates on CompassPlaybook.com. Experiment with a variety of recording tools and see how each one brings about different breakthroughs.

If you can think it,
you can have it,
live it, or be it.

It's all up to you.

SECTION ONE:
UNDERSTANDING COMPASS

What COMPASS Does

COMPASS Playbook provides a framework to conjure your most important aspirations, clarify their exact details, and focus your attention on their attainment. It's a breakthrough tool in easily achieving the success you want.

You will come to trust your ability to create the life you want, exactly the way you want it using the Playbook.

COMPASS proposes a simple formula:

Belief + Focus = Fulfilled Desire

What that means is that when we **believe** that our desire is attainable and keep positive **focus** on the end result, we quickly and enjoyably **fulfill that desire**.

It's that simple.

Often we don't experience it that easily, which is where COMPASS comes in. Within this framework lies a process to gently shift your understanding so the formula works powerfully for you.

Understanding how to achieve our dreams is often a struggle because we:

- Are unclear about what we truly desire
- Are unsure that we can even attain our desires
- Are not in control of our thoughts

- Inadvertently focus on what we *don't* want
- Doubt our worthiness

COMPASS dispels misconceptions about desire, thoughts and beliefs and offers new, powerful processes for getting what you want. It shows you how to take charge of your thinking and apply intentional focus, allowing for inspired action to help you attain your aspirations faster and with more satisfaction.

The COMPASS framework uses the mind-engaging activities of writing, drawing, mind mapping, visualizing and storyboarding in the form of *Plays*. These Plays help you practice new thinking behaviors that orient your focus toward attaining your most important aspirations.

After starting COMPASS, you will not only be closer to fulfilling your desires, but you'll find the journey a richer, more engaging experience.

What COMPASS Delivers

It's up to you what you get out of COMPASS. You discover it. You define it. You design it. You ignite it.

People who have used the COMPASS framework have experienced:

- Breakthroughs in achieving their most important aspirations
- More inner peace
- Greater enjoyment of the journey
- Pleasant, unexpected insights
- Improved relationships and deeper compassion
- Increased trust in life and the natural process of creativity

What will it deliver for you? That's entirely up to you. That's the elegance of COMPASS.

Let's Get Started

STICK FIGURES ENCOURAGED

To make the most of your COMPASS experience, suspend subjective criticism regarding your artistic or writing ability. This is not about how well you draw or write. The more natural and at ease you are while doing each Play, the more effective the experience will be for you.

Draw like you did when you were five years old. Use colors, pictures, and textures. Draw what's in your heart. Be fully self-expressed and enjoy playing. The more childlike and loose you are, the more profound your realizations will be. It's your Playbook. It's your private space to create the world *you* see—to scribble, doodle, scratch, cartoon, paint, paste, and write anything you want.

The act of drawing even the simplest rudimentary image stimulates areas of the brain that connect us to our higher mind and allow us to *really* see. It is an act of true creation: bringing forth that which was not before. It helps us define and clarify the details of what we desire, which helps us create a stronger, lifelike focus that attracts the perfect resources and inspires us to action.

OPEN YOUR MIND

The best way to approach COMPASS is with an open mind. Tell your inner critic to take a break during your time with COMPASS. It is a private time for you to create, reflect, and engage your innermost desires. What you create while engaged with COMPASS is precious!

COMPASS Plays introduce ways of processing thoughts and ideas that we're not normally used to. They sometimes stir the complaint cocktail, which may get in the way of a real breakthrough. When that happens, say, "Thank you for sharing," and put the complaining voice aside. It's likely fear-based negative thinking, and there's no place for that while you are sculpting and defining the happy, exciting future you desire.

DOGMA AND FINGER-WAGGING

The COMPASS Playbook is not about religion or morality. There is no right or wrong, because you define it as you use it. It is a framework of intentional thought that empowers you to be the designer of your aspiration and to have greater enjoyment on the journey toward its attainment.

'IT IS WHAT IT IS'

We are so used to defining and rationalizing the

effectiveness of something that we can lose sight of why we're doing it in the first place. The **COMPASS** Playbook is a cumulative engagement of activities that helps you experience a shift in generating what you want. It is specifically crafted for you to take and make your own.

THE PAST IS THE PAST

Contrary to popular belief, there is no need to heal the past. When we "heal ourselves," we reactivate the energy of that past experience and bring it into our present moment, which can negatively influence our thoughts and emotions. If our thoughts move us toward what we want, yet we're focused on what we *don't* want (how we feel about a past experience, for example), we'll never get to where we really want to be.

All that you have experienced has been part of your creative life journey. Appreciate your past choices for having brought you to this moment of discovery. The way you feel right now is all that matters, and every new moment can bring freshness and aliveness, if you let it.

Everything that you've experienced in the past is complete. Everything that you are today is perfect and as it should be. Making peace with the past and moving on, so to speak, is as simple as making peace with the past and moving on. Period.

HAVE FUN OR GO HOME

The **COMPASS** Playbook is to be used in a spirit of fun and exploration. The more imagination, creative thinking, colors, textures, whimsy and goofiness you bring to each Play, the more your mind will open up to exciting possibilities.

We are trained problem solvers. Our minds are wired to resolve the *how* of everything we attempt. When we were kids, we didn't care. We just played. **COMPASS** works best when you defer judgment, trust that **COMPASS** will deliver, and let your inner kid come out to play.

Engaging the Brain with the Creative Process

Storytelling. Drawing. Visualizing. Your full personality, energy and desire is embedded within these very personal, creative activities. It's the beginning of the creative process, the first step toward designing the details of the world you want.

STORYTELLING

The act of writing, storytelling, scripting and using language to express our feelings stimulates parts of the brain hungry for self-expression. How you tell the story of your aspiration is the first step in the process of bringing it forth with all the details and preferences that you select.

DRAWING

Hand-drawn images engage a different part of the brain and inspire realizations that words alone cannot. To draw your aspiration requires seeing it differently. You will experience unexpected breakthroughs in understanding the true potency of your aspiration through the simple act of drawing.

VISUALIZING

If you imagine, you visualize. If you dream, you visualize. It's like using the mind as a canvas or a movie screen to define your aspirations. In visualization, you are not limited to two-dimensional output. Visualizing has all the sensory characteristics of real life and is often the most gratifying process in the **COMPASS** Playbook.

Used in collaboration, these three creative activities engage your full mind, making developing and defining aspirations a richly textured experience.

The Six Premises

COMPASS functions on six distinct premises. Understanding these premises will make the creative processes resonate with you and heighten your personal insights. In addition, you'll quickly see how your thinking impacts everything you want, get, or don't get.

PREMISE 1 - DESIRE

A desire is a pulling sensation occurring deep within ourselves, birthed from something we perceive as missing or incomplete. Desire is an attraction to tangible or intangible experiences; it is the origin or catalyst of all aspirations. Moment by moment, the living of life provides a bounty of experiences that trigger new desires. In a living human being, desire is endless.

Examples of desire are: to want, to yearn for, to require, to wish for, to be eager for, to long for, to crave, to hunger for, etc.

There are nearly endless ways to satisfy a desire, which is why clarification is crucial to discovering how or what may best satisfy it. Most of us get caught up in the solution before we take the time to really understand our desires, which is one reason we fail to satisfy them.

PREMISE 2 - ASPIRATION

Simply put, an aspiration is the fulfillment of a desire. This is the result that satisfies what was originally perceived as missing or incomplete. It is brimming with detail and criteria defined by the desirer.

Examples of an aspiration are: a new start-up, a second home, a sexier car, a vacation in Hawaii, a leaner body, learning a second language, getting an advanced degree, eliminating hunger in your community, raising funds for a needy charity, having a closer relationship with a loved one, paying off your mortgage, etc.

A variety of aspirations can satisfy a single desire. It depends on personal preferences and how well personal beliefs support the aspiration. (Substitute the words dream, wish, goal, objective for aspiration if that helps.)

PREMISE 3 - BELIEF

A belief is an idea, notion or concept that we agree or disagree with. Deconstructed, a belief is merely a thought we have adopted as a personal truth through repetition and reinforcement. Beliefs are powerful because we allow them to influence whether we attain our aspirations or not. This thinking works for us or against us and what we want.

Examples of beliefs are: I will get a cold if I go out in the rain without a jacket; I am too old to get my PhD; I'm not good at math; I'm great at sales; cancer runs

in my family so I'll likely get it; I am or I'm not smart/ strong/good-looking enough; I don't know the right people to get ahead, etc.

Because we rarely question our beliefs, we unconsciously allow them to be the decider of our success or our failure. Now that we know that, we can consciously choose to modify our beliefs so they support what we want.

PREMISE 4 - FOCUS

Focus is the intentional act of directing the mind to a specific topic. When a topic is focused upon, attention and energy are concentrated on that topic. This amplifies the topic's energy and attracts cooperative influences.

Examples of focus are: Giving attention to your ideal weight, seeing yourself getting the new job, visualizing the new company in full operation, thinking only about enjoying your relationship with a new mate, adding more details to your specific aspiration, etc.

Focus is a deliberate act we choose once we've declared an aspiration. By focusing on our aspiration in its end state, complete with every detail, we engage and excite our mind and emotions, which leads the way to inspired action.

PREMISE 5 - INSPIRATION

Inspiration is an unexpected thought that excites us, supports and pulls us toward our aspiration. Whereas motivation is conscious maneuvering away from something unwanted (requires effort), inspiration is unconscious ideation that arrives unexpectedly from endless sources (is effortless).

We love being inspired! Inspiration, when it hits us, is like nothing else. It has the power to reinvigorate a stalled idea or invent a brave new one. Everyone has access to inspiration because it's a natural ability we're all born with.

Examples of inspiration are: a gut feeling to take a different route to work and finding out you avoided a major accident, a flash of brilliance on how to solve a complex problem, an insight that makes you go to an event where you meet your future spouse, or a spontaneous thought that stirs you to create an exceptional work of art, etc.

The value of inspiration is when we are open and listening for it. When it comes, we want to use it to inspire us to act in such a way that moves us closer to our aspiration. Inspirations that make us feel good, excited and eager are inspirations we should act upon because they are sourced from our desire.

PREMISE 6 - EMOTION

Our feelings are pivotal to indicating if we're focused on our aspiration or not. Because our emotion comes from the same inner place our desire comes from, it is the meter of our progress toward achieving our aspiration, thus satisfying our desire.

Examples of emotions are: joyful, eager, resigned, bored, satisfied, calm, etc.

In **COMPASS**, emotions are the direct link to whether you are focused on your aspiration or not. The more positive the emotion, the more you are focused on the right things and on the right track.

Retraining the Mind

COMPASS helps retrain your mind to focus on what you *do* want and away from what you *don't* want. It is the practice of intentional thinking, a method of consciously directing thought that not only makes you feel better, but aligns you with satisfying your most important desires.

In the beginning, there is desire. You shape and adjust your desire based on personal preferences, often unconsciously. This thought process awakens certain beliefs about achieving your aspiration, and those beliefs are held as the truth. This set of beliefs orients your focus to whether or not you can attain your aspiration, which is metered by your emotions.

For example, you have desire, and you have beliefs. When you doubt the attainment of your desire because of your beliefs, you experience negative emotions such as depression, frustration and resignation. With negative beliefs, there is a tendency to dwell on drawbacks, shortcomings, lack of training/experience, inability to solve how to "get there," thus attracting what you don't want: failure of attaining your aspiration.

Those who foster positive beliefs around their desire attract inspired action and the attainment of their aspiration. You know these people. They are the success stories, the change makers, the people who think big and get things done. To their core, they truly believe

they can succeed. As a result, it's easy for them to focus on the desire being attained because they believe it's possible.

The key here is focus. Most of us don't realize we can change our beliefs by changing our thinking.

But what are beliefs?

They are ideas, concepts or notions we agree or disagree with and hold as a personal truth until we say otherwise.

But what are ideas, concepts or notions?

Thoughts.

Hence, if beliefs are really just thoughts we've chosen to agree or disagree with, then we can change them.

See how we're really the ones in control here?

Now hold on a minute, you say. Change our thoughts? Not as easy as you think, right?

Those of you who may be unfamiliar with intentional, focused thought about attaining what you want may need guidance in the beginning. Enter **COMPASS**. This Playbook Companion provides processes that help your thoughts migrate to more purposeful, aspiration-centric thoughts.

When we intentionally hold our focus on our aspiration, we feel better. Surprisingly, we also enjoy the journey more profoundly. We open ourselves to insights that inspire us to action. And when we achieve our aspiration, there's nothing more satisfying, because

we know deep down that we were the creators from the very beginning.

The Framework

The COMPASS Play framework is presented in three distinct parts: Inquiry, Messenger and Bond. Each part has a specific purpose, and each complements the other in creating results that generate consistent breakthroughs.

INQUIRY

Inquiry is about heightening the clarity around what you want. Inquiry Plays involve divergent ideation where you imagine, brainstorm and create lists. Inquiry Plays are about accessing and giving center stage to what interests you most. Inquiry Plays are just that: deep inquiries into why you want what you want in the way you want it, as well as explorations into the endless ways to define its characteristics.

MESSENGER

Messenger is about freeing your inner five-year-old. It's where your ideas become real visual representations in your mind and on paper. You draw, mind-map, write, storyboard, visualize, scribble, doodle, color, and script your aspirations with all of their nitty-gritty details. Messenger Plays stimulate the whole brain and are responsible for the F-U-N in COMPASS. Messenger

Plays are also where most of the breakthroughs occur, especially as you draw the world you see in your mind and feel in your heart.

BOND

Bond seals the deal. Bond Plays help you sustain and embed all that you are discovering with COMPASS. Bond Plays show you how to open yourself to fresh insights, aha moments and bursts of inspiration. It shows you how to quickly convert these sparks into action and get yourself closer to attaining your aspirations.

All of the COMPASS Plays complement and build upon one another. However, if you feel you need to clarify your idea more, do an Inquiry Play. If you want to shape your idea and flesh out some of its details or criteria, do a Messenger Play. And if you are struggling with when to take action or how to align your focus and improve how you feel, do a Bond Play.

Making the Most of COMPASS

The 52 COMPASS Plays are fairly straightforward. Each Play has step-by-step instructions, and some include additional coaching. These Plays are intended to be re-Played over and over. Use them for all types of different aspirations, at different periods throughout your life, or on different areas you want to focus on such as professional, personal, relationships, spiritual, financial, community, career, or health and well-being.

If the inner critic starts to creep in, time your Plays. Set them to 5, 10 or 15 minutes in length to do, and it will help you stay focused. The faster your pen moves (or fingers if you're typing), the more clearly you'll hear desire-based thoughts.

Before long, these Plays will become second nature. They are designed to be free-flowing and open; customize them and the Playbook however you want—that's what makes COMPASS work so well.

Capturing Inspirations

Each **COMPASS** Play is fairly self-explanatory. For first-timers, follow the numerical order of the Plays to thoroughly maximize your experience.

Inspiration will increase in frequency and quality—a great by-product of using **COMPASS**—and best practice is to have more than one method for capturing your random ideas, insights and aha moments.

Here are a few suggestions:

- Paper and pen is the best. Invest in additional mini notebooks or something similar to supplement the main recording tool you are using with your **COMPASS** Playbook Companion.
- Call a friend and have them take down your inspiration/idea or leave it on their voicemail. It's even better if they are also using the Playbook, as you can be part of the **COMPASS** Community (see Appendix) and support each other's ideation process.
- Dictation device or digital recorder.
- Use your mobile phone's recording or note-taking application, or you can email the inspiration to yourself.
- A computer or tablet device is always great, especially for storing and categorizing ideas.

Take a few minutes and make a list of ways you

can capture your insights. Consider your activities throughout the day, places you frequent, and think of ways you can instantly capture ideas when they come.

When you're finished, pick one or two from your list and set up those capturing methods.

Now that your capturing methods are set, make a list of ways you can incorporate "open space" into your day so you can catch those insights when they come. Open space is quiet time, meditation, or a simple walk in nature—solitary time for you and your thoughts.

Try to incorporate at least one of those moments into each day. If life's demands prevent it, don't worry. Insights will find their way to you. Open space just allows them to come to you faster. They will arrive sooner than you expect, so be ready.

Creative Processes

WRITE

When asked to write as part of a Play, you can do any type of writing that's comfortable for you. Some prefer one-word bullet points or a simple list. Others write elaborate prose or journal-type storytelling that's a straight stream-of-consciousness from deep within. The more honest and authentic you are, the more rewarding it is. Unexpected breakthroughs often happen hours or even days after you've expressed yourself through the written word.

Writing also includes scripting, either as dialog or from someone else's point of view (POV). Feel free to use a standard dialog format of quotations, or just break each spoken word or sentence on its own line for better readability. Point of view refers to writing from someone else's perspective. What would they say about you or your aspiration? How would they answer that question? You can write in "their voice" as you connect with how you perceive what they are thinking or what they would say.

Much of your writing and scripting will call upon your ability to imagine the world you want, complete with all the details you assign. It's like a party for your imagination!

STORYBOARD

Used in animation, commercials and movie making, this drawing process represents graphical events or scenes in linear time. Storyboarding uses a grid of squares to display pivotal segments in a time span. In COMPASS, storyboarding uses a six-square grid, and the drawings inside each box indicate a stage or step in a process over time, or a series of individual snapshots. These drawings can be as simple or complex as you want them to be. Lay out each storyboard so it fits the proportion and size of your sketchbook or journal.

MIND MAP

Start in the center of the page and write one or two words that describe the essence of your aspiration or idea in a circle. Brainstorm aspects of that aspiration or idea, things that are influenced by it, touch it, or are required components of it. As you do, write them down and connect each to the aspect that inspired it with a line.

For example, if you write NEW CAR in the center, stem out with words like BMW, blue, sports package, insurance, gas, garage, window tinting, freedom, lease, commute, look good, reliability, license plate, fast, tire package, etc. As one word or group of words stimulates another, connect those together. Before you know it, you've acknowledged the many aspects of your

aspiration or idea, making it more real for you.

DRAW

Refer to the FYO (Five-Year-Old) Play to really understand how to draw with COMPASS. The more uninhibited you are, the more revealing the drawing will be. The last thing you want to do is get hung up on the "quality" of your drawing. It's not about that. It's about feeding the part of your brain stimulated by imagery. You'll be surprised how drawing can create some of the most potent breakthroughs around your desires and aspirations. Stick figures. Lines. Circles. Smiley faces. Draw like you were five years old and use color, texture and whatever you want, as long as it's pictures and imagery.

If you're feeling particularly adventurous and have access to kid's toys, you can also do drawing Plays using Lego®, Play-Doh, building blocks, dolls, toy cars, or any craft/hobby materials.

ACTIVITY

An activity Play involves an action or a behavior. Whether it's re-reading positive statements to yourself before bed, changing up an aspect of your work routine to increase spontaneity, or reorganizing how your day flows, activities help reinforce the Plays and add more

quality to your life.

These physical behaviors also help imprint the mind with new patterns of thinking, reinforcing the power of COMPASS.

VISUALIZE

Another ability we learned as kids is to visualize. Our imaginations ran wild with daydreaming, imagining and visualizing make-believe adventures and activities. COMPASS Plays that use visualizing techniques are no different.

Depending on the Play, a visualization can take place anywhere you can find a quiet place where you will not be disturbed for a short period of time. Sit in a comfortable chair or lie down with your eyes closed and relax. Following the Play's steps, create a mental image or a movie in your mind's eye. Visualizations are soothing for some and stimulating and exciting for others. You get to mentally experience all of the sensory inputs (smell, touch, hear, taste, see) of what you are visualizing, and it is highly satisfying.

The visualizing creative process is applicable to every Play, so feel free to do a visualization as a "bonus" step for each one. It will help reinforce the aspiration you're developing.

CREATIVE PROCESS KEY

Each Play has a graphic icon that gives you a quick glance at what creative process is used. Here is the corresponding key for quick reference:

W = Write

S = Storyboard

M = Mind Map

D = Draw

A = Activity

V = Visualize

SECTION TWO:
INQUIRY PLAYS

PLAY 1: FYOs Rock!   W A

1. Write at the top of the Play page: "Five-Year-Olds Are:"

2. List the characteristics, behaviors, and qualities of a five-year-old (FYO) child. These are even more powerful if they are qualities *you* had as a five-year-old (e.g. spirited, innocent, goofy, inventive, in-the-moment, curious, etc.).

3. In a second list, write the ways you can incorporate FYO qualities from your first list into your daily routine and your overall attitude.

COACHING

Always allow your inner FYO to come forth when you use COMPASS.

PLAY 2: Selfish Pleasures   W A

1. Make a list of the things you do, or would like to do, to spoil, soothe or enjoy yourself. These are "feel-good" activities involving foods, fun experiences, indulgences, mental and physical getaways, purchases, new things, or socializing with people you like. If the item or activity on your list answers the question: "Does doing this activity/thing make me feel better?" it qualifies as a Selfish Pleasure, no matter how seemingly insignificant it is.

2. When you're feeling low or having negative thoughts or doubts, do a Selfish Pleasure from your list.

3. Evolve this list over time as you think of more ways to soothe and enjoy yourself.

COACHING

As additional idea prompts, note what Selfish Pleasures come to mind when you think of these concepts: bask, drink, outside, laughter, music, community, family, quiet, entertainment, artistic, creative, play, travel, friends, animals, learning, peace, nature, food, solitude.

Feeling good is pivotal to COMPASS success, so enjoy your Selfish Pleasures!

PLAY 3: Feeling Meter   D W

1. Draw a thermometer or ruler on the left side of the page. Make it big enough to have 10 equal increments.

2. Number the increment points from 1 to 10 starting at the bottom.

3. Select and assign 10 emotional states you identify with and regularly experience. Assign the lowest, or most negative, emotion to the 1 point at the bottom. Assign the highest, or most positive, emotion to the 10 point. Assign your other emotions to correlate with the other eight points, low to high.

4. This is your Feeling Meter. Familiarize yourself with what number correlates to what emotion as you'll be checking in with yourself on a regular basis using this measuring tool. As your future emotions evolve, you may want to revisit this Play and establish a new set of feeling points.

COACHING

The key here is that *you* decide the "10" emotion, the "7" emotion, etc. Pay particular attention to the location of your feeling point. Increase your awareness of where you are on the Feeling Meter. This will become an invaluable tool as you use COMPASS. In fact, check in

before each Play and note the number corresponding to how you feel, and track how COMPASS helps improve your emotional state.

To help get you started, here are common emotions or emotional qualities. Pick the ones that suit how you typically feel, and correspond them to the point you choose on your Feeling Meter, or write your own. (Notice how each word has its own distinct *energy*.)

Agitated, agony, agreeable, amenable, angry, anguish, animated, anxious, apathetic, appreciation, assertive, awake, balanced, beaten, blessed, bliss, bored, bothered, buoyant, calm, cheerful, childlike, chipper, comforted, complacent, compliant, content, cynical, delighted, depressed, despair, discouraged, disgusted, disappointed, disturbed, doubtful, dreamy, eager, ebullient, ecstatic, elated, empowered, enchanted, energized, enlivened, enraptured, enthusiastic, excited, exhilarated, exuberant, fearful, fired up, flat, flexible, free, frustrated, furious, glad, grateful, gratified, grief, guilty, happy, heartened, hopeful, horrified, hurt, impatient, indifferent, innocent, insecure, inspired, interested, intrigued, irate, irked, irritated, jazzed, jealous, jolly, joyful, jubilant, light, lively, lost, loved, miserable, neutral, offended, optimistic, overwhelmed, pain, passion, passive, peaceful, perky, pessimistic, philosophical, pissed-off, pleasant, pleased, pliant, powerful, powerless, pressured, proud, provoked, rage,

refreshed, resentful, resigned, resilient, resistant, sad, satisfied, sentimental, sorrow, sparked, special, spirited, stimulated, stressed, strong, subdued, tenderness, terrorized, thrilled, tickled, tired, tormented, troubled, unbalanced, uncomfortable, uninspired, unworthy, upbeat, vengeful, warmth, weak, weary, worried, yearning.

Life causes us to be all over the emotional spectrum, sometimes from moment to moment. It's one of the wonderful things about being human. The key here, however, is that knowing our feeling point helps us understand where our thoughts are focused. The more positive your emotion (the higher the number), the more you are focused on your aspiration and what you want. When purposely focused on your aspiration, you are more open and available to insights, aha moments, blasts of brilliance, intuition, and ideas that lead to inspired action, as explained in the sixth COMPASS premise on emotion.

PLAY 4: Appreciation

1. Write an issue at the top of the page, specifically the one that is bothering or frustrating you.

2. Make a list of the things you appreciate about this issue. Look at it from all angles and possibilities. Consider it objectively and lovingly.

3. Replay as often as needed to bump your Feeling Meter point and raise your mood.

COACHING

Use this Play to help you through those moments when what you see isn't what you want and your Feeling Meter point is lower than you want it to be.

When you acknowledge and draw your focus to positive aspects of any person, situation or object, your feelings soften. The more you give your attention to what you don't like or don't want, the more things stay the same or worsen. The loving act of appreciation will neutralize any negative emotion and allow you to relax and turn your focus back to your aspiration.

This process is the most powerful Play in COMPASS.

PLAY 5: Aspirations   W

1. List all of the things you want to be, do, or have right now.

2. Recommended time for this Play is :05 minutes if you wish to time it.

3. Feel free to add to this list as additional ideas come to you.

PLAY 6: Aspiration Clarifier   M

1. Pick one aspiration that resonates with you from the previous Play and write it in the center circle.

2. Create a mind map of the aspects your aspiration generates, and connect each one to the aspect or idea that triggered it. Moving outward, fill the page with as many as you can.

COACHING

Mind mapping is a great way to clarify your aspiration. It also exposes the different ways to focus as well as concepts for future ideation. Mind maps use a true stream of consciousness that is highly effective at expanding many of the aspects of your idea or aspiration.

PLAY 7: Data Gathering   W   A

1. List the free and accessible things that you can do, research or learn to get closer to your aspiration. For example, if you want a new car, your list would include visiting car websites, taking note of cars you like driving around town, selecting a few and going for test drives, interviewing people who own the car you like, etc.

2. Plan and do at least one item from your list, more as appropriate or when you feel inspired to act.

3. Make note of your findings and use them in any of your Messenger Plays.

PLAY 8: More or Less

1. Think of something you would like more of, or less of, in your life. For example, "I would like more time to get my shopping done," or "I would like less frustration when I do my taxes."

2. Write a story about how your life would look with more of, or less of, that thing.

3. Note any insights you receive afterward.

PLAY 9: Unlimited Resources   W

1. Imagine you have access to all the resources/money/
    time necessary. What would you do, be or create?
    In other words, if there were no barriers to fulfilling
    an aspiration, what would it be?

2. Create that list. Don't worry about evaluating or
    considering the "how" of each item, just capture the
    ideas as fast as you can.

3. Review your list and select one idea that resonates
    with you.

4. Expand on this idea by writing about its completed
    state.

5. Write about how it makes you feel.

PLAY 10: Ultimate Career

1. If it paid whatever you wanted and provided all the perks you wanted, what ideas would you have for your ultimate career?

2. Create your ultimate career idea list, and hush your inner critic and the "how-to guy" as you do this Play.

3. Look at the list and select one idea that resonates with you.

4. Expand on this idea by writing about its completed state: you enjoying your ultimate career.

5. Write about how that makes you feel.

PLAY 11: Angel Investor

1. If an angel investor gave you a blank check and "no restrictions" to start any business, what would you start?

2. List your ideas. Hush the inner critic and the "how-to guy" if necessary.

3. Review your list and select one idea that resonates with you.

4. Expand on the idea by writing a story about it as if it's in full production, complete with infrastructure, operations, staff, customers and supply vendors. Include all the details of the community you serve, the difference you're making, and what role you play in the business.

5. Write about how that makes you feel.

PLAY 12: Goodies   D

1. If money, time or logistics were no issue, what material goodies, things, trinkets, stuff, bling, experiences, toys or trips would you want to create, build or buy?

2. Draw these things as creatively and in as much detail as you prefer.

3. Add more goodies to your drawings as they come to you.

PLAY 13: Globe Trekker   D

1. Putting money, time and logistics aside, think of the places around the world you would like to visit or live.

2. Draw the places you want to visit or live. Keep your drawings simple. As an option, draw icons you feel best represent those places. For example, for Key West, you could draw a conch shell; for Positano, Italy, you could draw a fiasco of Chianti or the winding coastal roads.

3. Add destinations as they come to you. If there is a destination that has a particular attraction or resonance for you, do a separate larger drawing or a collage that expands on the image. Make sure you are part of the picture!

PLAY 14: Preference Shaping

1. Consider an aspiration you are developing.

2. List the preferences of the aspiration in general terms. For example, if your aspiration is to buy a new condominium, some preferences could be top floor, private entrance, garage, new construction, etc.

3. Write separately where each preference came from. Describe the impetus for the preference as well as what you've augmented about it. For the new condominium, the preference of a garage may have been derived from the fact that your last apartment or home had no garage. As a result, you tolerated an exposed car and no storage space for your growing surplus of sports equipment.

4. When complete, think about how those experiences that, in the moment, you felt were bad or unlucky, were really helping you create a new and better future.

5. Note any thoughts or insights that come to mind.

PLAY 15: Life Experiences   S

1. Think of the things that happened to you or that you observed that have helped stir the desire that developed your aspiration.

2. As single snapshots, storyboard those events.

3. Acknowledge them for their value and thank them for occurring, for they brought you to where you are in your desires today. Know that life is, indeed, good.

COACHING

Life experiences stir desire and develop the details of our aspirations. They are important to acknowledge for their role in our growth. Remember to look at them closely.

PLAY 16: Wouldn't it be Nice if... W

1. Write a list of things you're noticing that you don't like, don't agree with, or just aren't happy with. Be careful not to lower your feeling point too much. If you find yourself getting a little negative or cranky, then quickly go to the next step.

2. For each thing you listed, brainstorm and list new aspirations that will solve or improve what you're dissatisfied with.

3. Keep expanding on your ideas over time, or create new aspirations altogether.

COACHING

COMPASS intentionally ignores negativity to avoid giving attention to what is unwanted. However, this Play can help you generate a slew of new aspirations from desires triggered by distasteful observations without staying in the spotlight of negativity. Use what you *don't* want as inspiration for what you *do* want.

SECTION THREE:
MESSENGER PLAYS

PLAY 17: Increments   S

1. In the first square of a storyboard, draw where you are today, and in the last square, draw a representation of your aspiration.

2. In the remaining four squares, draw what you imagine the interim stages would be on your way to your aspiration.

3. On a new storyboard, draw *different* snapshots of stages you imagine could happen on your way to your aspiration.

4. Repeat until you move to a higher feeling point.

COACHING

Use when you feel overwhelmed by the "how" of achieving your aspiration. This Play is about relaxing the pressure of attainment and acknowledging the increments of the journey. When using COMPASS, the "how" will naturally unfold through inspiration, ideas and insights. And, if they make you feel good when they hit you, take action.

PLAY 18: Belief Barrier   M

1. Write your aspiration in the center circle.

2. Create a mind map of the negative beliefs and/or doubts that arise when you think about attaining your aspiration.

3. Pay attention to what feelings come up as you do this Play.

COACHING

Use to uncover negative beliefs or doubts that may be a potential barrier to attaining your aspiration. This tool sets the stage for additional Plays on beliefs. Do the Belief Turnaround Play next.

PLAY 19: Belief Turnaround   W

1. Pick a negative belief from the Belief Barrier Play that resonates with you the most. Write it down as a statement (e.g. "I don't have the knowledge regarding how to start a new business, so I shouldn't").

2. Write a new statement that is rephrased to be more general or more positive (e.g. "I'm looking forward to learning more about starting a new business" or "I know how to have fear and still move forward").

3. Re-read the new belief statement and write about the experience you're having rephrasing the belief. Notice the degree of struggle or ease around your aspiration.

4. Repeat steps 1-3 for the other negative belief statements, and remember to focus on the positive.

COACHING

Use to further deconstruct beliefs uncovered in the Belief Barrier Play. This is where you begin the shifting process from a negative belief or doubt that holds your aspiration at bay, to a positive belief that frees the possibility of attaining your aspiration. Do the Belief Celebration Play next.

PLAY 20: Belief Celebration M W A

1. Write your aspiration in the center circle.

2. Create a mind map of the positive beliefs and attributes of your aspiration, as well as the good things that will come out of it when it's attained (e.g. "I have years of experience and know this industry well").

3. On a new page, list at least ten more refined positive statements that you accept and believe about your aspiration (e.g. "I am outgoing and people enjoy doing business with me" or "I really want to take care of my customers and gain great satisfaction helping them").

4. Every morning, read your refined positive statements that you accept and believe about your aspiration. This is more powerful if done out loud in front of a mirror.

COACHING

Use to celebrate the positive beliefs you accept about attaining your aspiration. Pay particular attention to how you feel as you move through this Play.

PLAY 21: Day in the Life   S

1. Storyboard a typical day in the life of your aspiration. For example, if your aspiration is to have a new bakery, you would draw in the first square opening your beautiful store early in the morning; the next square would be excitedly planning the menu for the day's baked items; the next would be you (or your employees) cheerfully making the cakes and goodies; the next would be eager patrons flowing in and out of your bakery, purchasing all of your fresh baked goods; the next would be you and your employees celebrating a successful day, and the final square would be you, satisfied and proud of your bakery's well-appreciated, profitable confectionery delights.

COACHING

This day-in-the-life Play can be storyboarded using a shorter segment of time or activity if you prefer (such as the process of baking and building a wedding cake), as long as there are six distinct states of that segment that you can storyboard. If you choose to do segments within a day, do additional storyboards so you get a full experience of your attained aspiration in its final state.

PLAY 22: Environment   D

1. Draw the environment, room, building, or outdoor space that holds your aspiration. For example, if your aspiration is a new catamaran, draw the sailboat with as much detail as you like with you at the helm, the inlet and waterways, the docks, the marina, bait shop, nearby boats, the people you'll sail with, trees, landscaping, buckets, ropes, fenders, pathways, the place you park your car when you drive to the marina, etc.

2. Be as detailed, colorful and explicit as possible, and include yourself in the scene. Remain loose and childlike in your drawing.

3. No written words, only drawing and imagery.

COACHING

Use to define (with as much detail as possible) the environment of your aspiration in its final state. This is a great Play to get more clarity around the personal preferences you are incorporating into your aspiration.

PLAY 23: The Five Senses   V W

1. Once comfortable, close your eyes and visualize your aspiration. When you have mentally centered on your aspiration, observe and immerse yourself in it using one of your five senses. Note how each sense conjures different emotions and sensations.

2. Do each visualization separately for sight, sound, smell, taste, and touch.

3. After each sensory visualization, write a short paragraph about the observations you made while visualizing as well as the overall experience. Adjust the details of your aspiration if needed.

COACHING

Use to further define your aspiration and its preferences through the five senses. It's not necessary to do all five sensory visualizations in one sitting, but they should be done independently of one another for a more visceral experience.

PLAY 24: Special Space   D W

1. Draw your ideal home, neighborhood, living space or office space. Choose a bedroom, a vacation home, an office or office building, or acreage at a country estate—whatever and wherever you want to make your special space.

2. Fill it with all of the things you want, and include yourself in the picture.

3. When your drawing is complete, write about a typical day enjoying your special space.

PLAY 25: Ideal Lifestyle   D   W

1. Draw a picture of your ideal lifestyle.

2. Include yourself and those you want surrounding you in your ideal lifestyle drawing.

3. When your drawing is complete, write a story that takes us through a typical day with you enjoying your ideal lifestyle.

PLAY 26: Day-Trips

S

1. Consider the moments between now and when you attain your aspiration.

2. Storyboard snapshots of fun, interesting and exciting experiences you would like to have along the way to your aspiration. These don't necessarily have to be moments of insight; they are strategic day-trips of exploration, discovery and simple pleasure. For example, you could meet a very interesting person who becomes a lifelong friend, or learn a new shortcut to work, or have a whole day to indulge in your favorite Selfish Pleasure.

PLAY 27: Emotional Excursion   W

1. Think deeply on your aspiration and what you'll be doing when you've attained it.

2. List the emotions associated with the activities and experiences you'll have after you've attained your aspiration, as if you were answering, "Now that I have [aspiration], I feel [emotion] while doing [activity or experience]." For example, if your aspiration is to buy a new Harley-Davidson motorcycle, you'd write: "Taking it over to my friend Steve's to show it off: Pride, joy. Riding my Harley on Route 1: exhilarating, relaxing, appreciation, lucky, happy, proud."

PLAY 28: POV

W

1. Imagine you have achieved your aspiration in its fullest detail and promise.

2. Think of a loved one, friend, mentor, or someone who cares deeply for your happiness.

3. From their point of view (POV), write how they'd describe you in the world of your attained aspiration. Have them talk about what you're doing, how you feel about it, and how it has improved your life.

PLAY 29: Anticipation W

1. Think of your aspiration.

2. Imagine the things, events, activities, people you'll meet, learnings, fun experiences, etc. that you are most looking forward to experiencing along the way to its attainment.

3. Write as many as you can, and note the associated feelings you have regarding each one.

COACHING

The more creative and inventive you are, the better. It's like forming mini-aspirations on the way to your big one. This is how you heighten the awareness of how joyful your journey can be as you travel to your aspiration, creating even greater anticipation.

PLAY 30: I'm So Excited!   W

1. In anticipation of your aspiration, what are you most excited about?

2. Regarding your aspiration, list the events, activities, steps in your journey, insights, aha moments, sharing with others, planning, researching and writing about that you are eagerly looking forward to experiencing.

PLAY 31: Well-Being

1. Regarding your aspiration, imagine that it has arrived.

2. Write about your personal physical, mental and spiritual well-being in this world of your attained aspiration. How are you feeling? What is your physical stamina and activity level? How much are you sleeping? What are you eating and drinking? How are you keeping your mind active? What does your body look like? What kind of clothes are you wearing? How are you keeping your heart happy and filled with joy and anticipation?

PLAY 32: Expansion   S W

1. Storyboard new aspects, elements, qualities or criteria that you can add to your aspiration. This may be challenging if you've already fleshed out your aspiration to the point you are happy with it. If so, try this Play anyway. It will help you open yourself to additional insights, and you may actually surprise yourself with something quite amazing.

2. List any insights or ideas for new aspirations. If you want to add any aspects you created in this Play to your existing aspiration, go ahead and do so.

COACHING

Aspirations are virtually endless in their scope and definition. It's up to you to decide what your aspiration looks like, down to the most minute detail. This Play allows you the freedom to develop new facets of your aspiration, even if it's just for fun.

PLAY 33: World Attitude   W

1. Imagine yourself in the state of your achieved aspiration.

2. What is your attitude about other people in your network, your community, the world? Write about it and note any insights that come to you.

PLAY 34: Community

W

1. Imagine your aspiration has arrived and you are enjoying every moment of it.

2. Write how you see people in your community benefiting from your aspiration and all it has brought about, whether it's the impact of your personal happiness, or how your new business stimulates the local economy and provides helpful goods and services to the public.

PLAY 35: Encouragers   W

1. Think of the people in your life who want the best for you: friends, mentors, your family, your professional network, your employer/employees.

2. Write about how these people are supporting and encouraging you in attaining your aspiration. Include how they believe in you, how they are getting caught up in the excitement you're generating, and how they are helping you stay the course by keeping you focused on your aspiration.

SECTION FOUR:
BOND PLAYS

PLAY 36: Focus Shifter   W

1. In a one-sentence statement, write the essence of the issue that's bothering you. For example, "I'm worried that I don't have enough smarts to go back to school and get my degree."

2. Write about why it came up or what triggered it. It could be an event, what someone said, a disappointment, doubt or limiting belief.

3. Write at least ten positive statements that neutralize the issue or at least make you feel better about it. Give yourself an inner pep talk, similar to how you'd cheer up a worried friend. Be general if it helps the believability of your new positive statement.

4. Lastly, write a positive statement concerning the issue, and that it has no more control over how you feel. Write how you're looking forward to feeling better and getting back on track to attaining your aspiration.

COACHING

Use when you're focused on something you don't want that's making your feelings or mood low.

PLAY 37: Spontaneity W A

1. List ways you can add spontaneity to your life.

2. Plan and do at least one method of spontaneity.

3. Add to this list over time. Regularly practice spontaneity to encourage inspired action.

COACHING

Ways of adding spontaneity include: a new way to work, eating a different type of food, calling someone you wouldn't have normally spoken to that day, giving yourself permission to change or postpone something previously scheduled.

You can even invite people to play along: "Hey, I'm incorporating spontaneity in my day and I'm going to change our lunch date to a play date. Let's see a movie!"

When we change our routines just a bit or try out new experiences, we create open space. This allows inspiration, insight, and new ideas to come to us because we are more sensory-aware. We see things anew. We let more joyful feelings in, especially if we are following our heart in our spontaneous decision to do something different.

PLAY 38: Great Things   W

1. List the positive things that will be available,
    created as by-products, or changed as a result of
    attaining your aspiration. As in, now that you've
    attained your aspiration, what's available to you?
    What's different? How are people/the community/
    the world impacted by what you've created?

2. Take one of the positive things from your list
    and expand it in story form. Sell the story of why
    that positive list item is a great thing now that
    you have attained your aspiration. For example,
    if your aspiration was to write and publish a
    romance novel, one positive list item might be,
    "I feel more accomplished because I completed a
    writing project." Your great things story would go
    something like, "Now that I've completed writing a
    novel, I have more confidence to take on additional
    writing projects. In fact, I have another idea for a
    new book, this one set as a historical romance," etc.

COACHING

Use this to reinforce the focus on your aspiration.
This speaks directly to the journey after your aspiration
is attained.

PLAY 39: Releasing the "How"   W

1. List the potential ways your aspiration can come to you. The more creative, bizarre, unexpected, whimsical, or abstract you are, the better. Yes, that means listing aliens landing and constructing your new house for you. (Well, maybe not *that* bizarre.)

2. Evolve this list. The more possible ways you can imagine your aspiration coming, the more you will relax the need to figure it out yourself. Before you know it, you'll be back on track with the right focus, and inspired action will take over. Have fun with it!

COACHING

Use this Play when you are preoccupied with the "how" of attaining your aspiration. We often worry about how we're going to get what we want because we're natural problem solvers and always in action. When this happens, all of our attention magnetically goes to the fact that we haven't yet achieved our aspiration. It can deplete our moods and increase impatience and frustration. By focusing on what's missing, we slow or stop the inspiration and aha moments from coming because we're focused on what we *don't* want.

PLAY 40: Impact   M

1. Write your aspiration in the center circle.

2. Create a mind map of the impact created by your aspiration. For example, if your aspiration is to have $100,000 by the end of the year, write about all of the things that will be possible, thus impacted, by that $100,000. For example, you could buy a lot of new toys, get free of debt, donate to your favorite charity, or create a new scholarship program.

COACHING

The purpose of this Play is to acquaint yourself with the impact created by your aspiration. It's not just about getting something. It's about how your aspiration will change the world and the people in it, even if it's just you. This adds a stronger attractive quality to the aspiration and it also helps you further develop or modify its characteristics.

PLAY 41: Inspirations   W A

1. Write how the next 24 hours will unfold for you. Include at least three occurrences of aha moments, bursts of brilliance, insights, gut feelings, mental pictures, or ideas that take you in a new direction regarding your aspiration.

2. When finished, reread it over the next 24 hours.

3. Make note of the inspirations that occur (and they will) over the next 24 hours.

COACHING

Use to help increase the occurrence of aha moments, inspiration and insights. This is a great way to train yourself to be open and in listening-mode for ideas that inspire action.

If you feel good when you get these inspirations, it's a sign to take inspired action, so move forward with the action. If you feel bad or worse, do a Play that will re-center you and get your focus back on track. Be wary of taking action when an insight makes you feel worse than you already do. In those cases, it's most likely the thought's origin is from a fear or negative belief.

PLAY 42: The Interview   W   A

1. Imagine yourself being interviewed by a journalist about your aspiration. Pretend you've already achieved your aspiration and answer these questions or invent your own:

    • What gave you this idea? Describe the journey getting to this moment.
    • What were some of the things you did to get here?
    • How does it feel to finally get here/achieve this?
    • What were some of the things you changed about it along the way?
    • What types of inspirations did you receive about this idea?
    • What does your [insert significant relationship here] think about it?
    • What's possible now that you've achieved this?

2. Write down any breakthroughs or aha moments you received while doing this Play.

3. Reread your interview any time your focus wanders away from your aspiration.

PLAY 43: Movement   W A

1. List the types of movement you really enjoy (e.g. walking, cycling, yoga, rowing, dancing, gardening, swimming, painting, etc.). The list criteria should include your body doing some kind of motion or activity.

2. Create opportunities to do movements from your list.

3. Note any insight or clarity that comes through while doing your movement.

COACHING

During physical movement, energy flows and the mind is temporarily caught up in what your body is doing. It's like an active meditation. Allow inspiration and ideas to come naturally to the surface as you enjoy your movement.

PLAY 44: Me-Time   A

1. Block off a day (or just 30 minutes for those with busy schedules) where you go completely off-grid for some "Me-Time." This is so you have the time period completely to yourself, free of obligations.

2. When the day (or time slot) arrives, begin your Me-Time by asking yourself, "What do I want to do right now?" and do it, no matter what it is.

3. When you're done that, ask yourself again, "What do I want to do now?" and do it, no matter what it is.

4. Repeat until your Me-Time has concluded.

5. Do this activity as frequently as possible.

COACHING

Take note of your emotions throughout your Me-Time. This can be a challenging Play for some people, because they are not used to allowing themselves to do what they want *when* they want. What's special about this Play is that our emotions typically improve because we have the luxury of being allowed to choose for ourselves.

- Take special note where your thoughts linger.
- What types of mental dreaming are you doing?

- What types of mental fretting are you doing?

When you catch yourself with a negative thought, acknowledge it and let it go. You don't have time for those unproductive thoughts during your Me-Time. Relax and enjoy doing exactly what you want.

PLAY 45: Head Trip   V W

1. In a visualization, take a mental trip to a favorite place, whether you've been there or not. Italy. The Caribbean. Your backyard. A jazz club. The beach. The moon.

2. While you are taking your mental trip, casually wander. Explore. Interact with things. Use all of your senses. Be a curious observer. Really feel the environment and how it embraces you.

3. While in this place, ask the question, "Tell me what I need to know today," and listen for answers.

4. When you're done with your visualization, write down any insights or answers you received. If you didn't receive any, don't worry. With regular practice, you will.

COACHING

The purpose of this Play is to put you in a state of relaxed pleasure as well as heightened sensory awareness. When you ask your question while in this relaxed state, you are more apt to receive the answer while in your favorite place. This is yet another process to help increase your listening for insights that inspire action.

PLAY 46: Mentor

1. Write down the names of five real or fictional people/figures/characters whom you admire or identify with and would be honored to receive advice from (e.g. Mother Teresa, Mark Twain, John F. Kennedy, Benjamin Franklin, Bugs Bunny, Superman, etc.).

2. With your eyes closed, ask a mentor, "What do I need to know about [your aspiration] today?"

3. Take a few moments to listen for their advice.

4. Write down what comes to your mind.

5. Repeat with each mentor.

PLAY 47: Project Completer W V D

1. Think of an unfinished or stalled project that you'd like to complete.

2. List answers to the question: "How many ways might the project be completed?"

3. After you finish the list, go back and after each item add time frames and any important details.

4. Visualize the project being completed.

5. Draw the project in its completed state.

COACHING

Use when you are distracted by an incomplete project. This Play relaxes any anxiety around your project. It helps you see alternative ways to get it moving forward so you can finish your project and start something new.

In addition, you, or any resources, don't *have* to do any of the items in your step 2 list. That is, unless you're inspired to do so. This should improve your attitude about the unfinished project and give you the freedom to complete it with greater enjoyment and satisfaction.

PLAY 48: Relationships

1. Think of a relationship you would like to improve and why.

2. Write a statement that describes the relationship state you would like to achieve. For example, "I would like to have a more trusting relationship with my son."

3. Write your aspiration as a positive statement in the present tense. For example, "I have a loving, open and trusting relationship of mutual respect with my son."

4. List as many things (tangible and intangible) that can happen to bring about your aspiration.

5. Allow insights to arrive naturally, and take inspired action when it feels good to do so.

COACHING

Use when you would like to improve a specific relationship with someone or some thing. For an extra bump, read the positive statements daily. For more stubborn interpersonal relationships, use the Appreciation Play in addition to this Play.

PLAY 49: Personal Aspect   W

1. Think of an aspect about yourself that you'd like to improve and why.

2. Write a statement that describes the enhanced or improved personal aspect that you want. For example, "I want to be a more patient person."

3. Write your aspiration as a positive statement in the present tense. For example, "My relationship with my son is much improved now that I am more patient and understanding of him and his needs."

4. List as many things (tangible and intangible) that can happen to bring about your aspiration.

5, Allow insights to naturally arrive, and take inspired action when it feels good to do so.

COACHING

Use when you have an aspect about yourself that you would like to enhance or improve. For an added bump, do the Appreciation Play, but appreciate *yourself*.

PLAY 50: Conversations   W

1. Pick a person whose opinion you value. It could be a loved one, a mentor, a friend, a hero, a leader, or a fictional character.

2. Write a dialog of you explaining your aspiration to them and why it's important to you. Include comments from them in a thoughtful dialog. Make sure that you ask them to help you develop the preferences about your aspiration.

3. When you're done writing, make note of any insights the conversation inspired.

PLAY 51: Inspiring Others   W

1. Imagine you have attained your aspiration and are enjoying everything it brought to you and your life.

2. Now that you have achieved it, write how you are sharing with and inspiring others through the living of your dream. How have you changed? How are you having a more pleasant impact on the people and relationships that are important to you? How is your excitement and joy influencing the lives of others? How are you the "ambassador of happy"?

3. Make a note of all inspirations that come to you.

COACHING

The people who love us just want us to be happy. And when we're happy, they're happy.

PLAY 52: What's Next?

W

1. Your aspiration has arrived. You are enjoying it fully. Think of a close friend or colleague and imagine them asking you, "I see you enjoying [your aspiration], and I'm happy for you. So, what's next?"

2. Write what you would say to them about any other aspirations that you may have.

3. Allow any insights for ideas about new aspirations to come and make a note of them.

APPENDIX: COMPASS RESOURCES

COMPASS Community

The **COMPASS** Community is a growing group of creators who actively use the **COMPASS** Playbook. As a Playbook user, you now have access to this community and can get even more out of your **COMPASS** experience.

This resource is all about *the art of sharing*. When you see what others are creating with their Playbooks, you will:

- Understand more about the intricacies of each Play
- Get more insights regarding the cultivation of your aspirations
- Improve your retention and focus
- Have the opportunity to contribute to others in a powerful way

In addition to the **COMPASS** Community, you'll have access to Playbook resources, support, creative process templates and additional Playbook content.

To join the **COMPASS** Community and learn more about Playbook resources, visit CompassPlaybook.com.

About the Author

Terry Pappy is a professional writer, designer and communications consultant. For 30+ years, she has helped organizations solve problems using authentic, creative and introspective techniques. She has inspired many to successfully incorporate people-centric, positive ideas into their business strategy.

After writing *14 Days*, she embarked on a campaign to transform the heart of business and its relationships—specifically in the customer channel—leveraging communications typically deployed through traditional marketing channels.

Terry also leads positive change through her COMPASS Playbook Write Shops, where participants are guided to new possibilities using their creative energy and imagination.

She lives in sunny Orlando, Florida.

www.ingramcontent.com/pod-product-compliance
Lightning Source LLC
Chambersburg PA
CBHW062001040426
42447CB00010B/1851